Sports Innovations

INNOVATIONS IN SOCCER

by Kristian R. Dyer

SportsZone
An Imprint of Abdo Publishing
abdobooks.com

abdobooks.com

Published by Abdo Publishing, a division of ABDO, PO Box 398166, Minneapolis, Minnesota 55439.

Printed in the United States of America, North Mankato, Minnesota.
102021
012022

THIS BOOK CONTAINS RECYCLED MATERIALS

Cover Photo: Carlos Sanchez Martinez/Icon Sportswire/AP Images, left; AP Images, right
Interior Photos: Lao qiang xa/Imaginechina/AP Images, 5; Pajor Pawel/Shutterstock Images, 6–7; Chris Lawrence/Alamy, 9; AP Images, 11; AFP/Getty Images, 12; Roland Witschel/picture-alliance/dpa/AP Images, 15; Matt Dunham/AP Images, 17; Jon Super/PA Wire/NMC Pool/Press Association/URN:54250455/AP Images, 19; Julian Avram/Icon Sportswire/AP Images, 21; Rich von Biberstein/Icon Sportswire/AP Images, 23; Martin Meissner/AP Images, 24; Mo Khursheed/TFV Media/AP Images, 26; Frank Hoermann/Sven Simon/picture-alliance/dpa/AP Images, 29; Mike Fiala/Getty Images Sport/Getty Images, 31; David Vincent/AP Images, 32; Ricky Carioti/AP Images, 35; George Peter Alexander Healy/Detroit Publishing Co./Library of Congress, 37; Thomas Kienzle/AP Images, 39; ullstein bild/Getty Images, 41; Robin Alam/Icon Sportswire/AP Images, 42; Dorn Byg/Cal Sport Media/AP Images, 43

Editor: Katie Chanez
Series Designer: Joshua Olson

Library of Congress Control Number: 2020949106

Publisher's Cataloging-in-Publication Data

Names: Dyer, Kristian R., author.
Title: Innovations in soccer / by Kristian R. Dyer
Description: Minneapolis, Minnesota : Abdo Publishing, 2022 | Series: Sports innovations | Includes online resources and index.
Identifiers: ISBN 9781532195068 (lib. bdg.) | ISBN 9781098215378 (ebook)
Subjects: LCSH: Soccer--Juvenile literature. | Technological innovations--Juvenile literature. | Sports sciences--Juvenile literature. | Performance technology--Juvenile literature. | Soccer--Equipment and supplies--Juvenile literature. | Sports--Juvenile literature.
Classification: DDC 688.76--dc23

TABLE OF CONTENTS

CHAPTER 1

A SIMPLE IDEA

Soccer is one of the simplest games ever invented: try to kick a ball into a goal. And indeed, it was one of the earliest known sports. Ball-kicking games date back to more than 2,000 years ago in China.

But these games didn't look much like the modern game of soccer. The rules were very different. The game of *cuju* in China involved two teams kicking a ball through a goal. But they had to keep the ball off the ground, and the goal was a hole in a net.

Other ball games emerged around the same time. The Greeks played one called *episkyros*. The Romans adapted this game and called it *harpastum*. This is the game that was said to have influenced the modern game of soccer in England. But that took many years.

caption: **The ancient Chinese game *cuju* is precursor to modern soccer. Entertainers still demonstrate the game today.**

The Cambridge University Football Club claims to be the oldest soccer club in the world still playing.

THE CAMBRIDGE RULES

The modern game of soccer, called football in many parts of the world, developed in England in the 1800s. Until then, soccer was similar to rugby, but it was also violent. Players often kicked each other more than the ball.

The game was popular on college campuses. And Cambridge University in Cambridge, England, was no different. However, one school's version of the game could be very different from another's. In 1848 a group of Cambridge students got together to make some rules. These were the first known rules of soccer.

Some of the 11 original rules were different from how the game is played today. Players could catch the ball and kick it again, for example. But many of the other rules were the same as today. These rules also banned the violent kicking of opponents and tripping that had become common.

WOMEN'S SOCCER

Women were playing soccer in the earliest days, too. By the early 1920s, women's games were beginning to attract big crowds. However, this proved problematic for the FA. Not wanting to draw attention away from the men, the FA barred women from its fields in 1921. Other nations enacted similar bans. It wasn't until 1969 that these began to be lifted.

Not every team adopted the Cambridge rules. Some clubs made their own. But soccer started progressing toward one modern game.

THE FOOTBALL ASSOCIATION

John Charles Thring was a student at Cambridge when the rules were developed. He then went on to become a teacher at the Uppingham School and remained involved in the development of the game. He revised the Cambridge Rules for Uppingham in 1862.

Thring's rules outlined infractions such as offsides and standardized the height of the crossbar for the goal. Thring was passionate about soccer and believed there should be a

A plaque in London commemorates the site where the FA was formed in 1863.

national association to govern the rules. In 1863 Thring sent his rules to the brand-new Football Association (FA).

The FA considered both the Cambridge rules and Thring's rules as it set to create one standard set of guidelines. One of the FA's founding members was Ebenezer Morley. As a player himself, Morley knew how violent soccer could be.

Morley agreed with Cambridge and Thring that violence had no place in the game. He drew up the first official rules of soccer. They were later published and called the "Laws of the Game." Morley played in the first match using the new rules in 1863.

Because England established the first official rules, it became the birthplace of modern soccer. The FA still governs soccer in England and is the oldest soccer organization in the world. But other countries soon joined.

FIFA

As soccer started to spread to other countries, international matches became popular. England and Scotland played the first international match in 1872. A new association was needed to be in charge of these matches.

The *Fédération Internationale de Football Association* (FIFA) formed in Paris on May 21, 1904. Seven countries were founding members. But England was not one of them. The FA felt that since it had invented modern soccer, it should be in charge. The FA eventually changed its mind and joined in 1905.

The existence of FIFA was challenged several times. World War I (1914–18) disrupted international soccer and hardly any matches were played. By the end of the war, FIFA had

FIFA governed international matches and eventually would go on to create the World Cup.

nearly collapsed. But co-founder Carl Hirschman worked to keep it alive. He rebuilt the organization after the war, almost completely on his own and at his own expense.

Soccer was first held at the Olympics in 1900 in Paris, France. In the sport's early days, the Olympic champion was considered the best in the world. And the Olympic soccer tournament proved particularly popular. In 1924, the gold-medal match drew 60,000 fans to Paris to watch Uruguay defeat Switzerland 3–0. With the popularity of international soccer, FIFA began to consider staging its own event.

Jules Rimet, *left*, founded the French Football Federation before serving 33 years as FIFA president

THE WORLD CUP

FIFA president Jules Rimet was the driving force behind organizing the new tournament. He reached out to member nations to get their input on the idea. On May 28, 1928, FIFA officially announced it would be staging a world championship. For a host, FIFA turned to two-time Olympic champion Uruguay. The tournament was scheduled for 1930.

Not every nation was excited to play. Europe was dealing with an economic crisis. The journey to Uruguay at that time was long and expensive. Many European countries, including England, declined to send their national teams.

In all, 13 teams made it to Uruguay, where all games were held. Nearly 93,000 fans came out for the final in Montevideo. Uruguay defeated Argentina 4–2 to become the first World Cup champion.

The World Cup was a historic moment for the game of soccer. It showed that soccer had become a global sport, and that great teams existed outside Europe. Today the World Cup is one of the most popular sporting events in the world. More than 3.5 billion people watched the 2018 World Cup final. That was more than half the population of the planet.

JULES RIMET TROPHY

For his role in creating the world's biggest soccer tournament, Jules Rimet is known as the "Father of the World Cup." His name was added to the World Cup trophy in 1946, becoming the Jules Rimet Cup. Rimet made a rule that the first nation to win the trophy three times got to keep it for good. Brazil achieved that in 1970, and a new trophy replaced it.

CHAPTER 2

CHANGING THE GAME

As soccer players got stronger and faster throughout the 1900s, the pace of play picked up as well. Players had less time to think and less space to work. One response to this progression was the creation of a playing style called total football. In total football, any player could play any position, and they could switch throughout a game.

This style of play became popular in Europe in the 1970s. The Dutch did not invent total football, but they did popularize it. It was commonly used in the Dutch league and by the men's national team of the Netherlands.

Total football was a revolutionary soccer thought. Previously, a forward was only expected to score goals, and a defender didn't have to be a strong passer or good at dribbling. The defender only had one job: to defend.

caption: **Johan Cruyff and the Dutch national team helped popularize total football during the 1970s.**

ANTI-FOOTBALL

Teams who are playing the opposite of total football are said to be playing anti-football. Rather than going all-out to win, teams playing anti-football play not to lose. They focus only on defense and physical play to frustrate their opponent. Dutch legend Johan Cruyff accused his former team of playing this way in the 2010 World Cup. For Cruyff, playing the game the right way was more important, even if the team lost.

Dutch defenders were creative and had strong passing skills. Midfielders such as Johan Cruyff were able to dribble and defend. Their forwards were complete players too. Even their goalkeepers could pass the ball well with their feet.

Other teams saw this style and tried to imitate it. Total football spread throughout the soccer world, especially after the Dutch national team made it to back-to-back World Cup finals in 1974 and 1978. Everyone wanted to play it.

TIKI-TAKA

Then in the early 2000s, the Spanish national team changed soccer again, bringing in a style called *tiki-taka*. The Spanish style embraced the idea of total football but added short passing and quick ball movement.

The name *tiki-taka* comes from a Spanish phrase meaning "quick steps." Short passes make for a fast, free-flowing style

Behind star midfielder Andrés Iniesta (6), Spain used the quick style *tiki-taka* to win the 2010 World Cup.

of play. It began with the great FC Barcelona teams of the 1980s and the 1990s. But *tiki-taka* took off when Spain's national team used the style on its way to winning the 2010 World Cup.

A MODERN MELD OF STYLES

More recently, the popular trend is pressing and counter-pressing. Gone are the days of patient build-ups when teams passed the ball and played keep-away from the opponent.

Today modern teams play quick and fast. They press their opponent back and try to force mistakes in front of the goal. Once the team loses the ball, its players begin counter-pressing, trying to chase the ball down. The system minimizes space for opposing teams, making it difficult for them to pass the ball.

Liverpool won the 2019–20 English Premier League title using a system that employs a high line of defenders. They create less space for play and press their opponent back, making it difficult to pass the ball. It is an exhausting style to play, but it can be effective. Teams such as RB Leipzig in Germany and Red Bull Salzburg in Austria have made this a devastating style to play against.

"Pressing and counter-pressing is all about making the opponent uncomfortable," said Red Bull Salzburg head coach, Jesse Marsch.

Marsch is the first US-born head coach to lead a team in the European Champions League. He's a true pioneer of American soccer. As head coach of the New York Red Bulls, he led the team to the best regular-season record in Major League Soccer (MLS) twice.

The way soccer is played varies and is always changing. That's part of the fun of soccer, seeing the different styles emerge and clash with each other. These different styles of play make soccer a unique game.

Defender Virgil van Dijk, *right*, was the key to Liverpool's success using a high-pressure defensive style.

CHAPTER 3

TECH IN SOCCER

Professional players practice a lot and play a lot of games. There is not much time to recover. Immediately after each game, they start the process of getting their bodies ready for the next game. Muscles have to heal and recover.

All high-level teams integrate nutrition and science in the recovery process. They employ trainers, nutritionists, and dieticians to work with their players. Few know and understand this better than Rick Guter, a longtime MLS and US national team athletic trainer. During the 2020 season, Guter worked for the Colorado Rapids.

"In the past, the day after a game, there may have been no activity," Gunter said. "Now most teams will have a 'recovery session' where the players might get together to do a jog or a stretch for 20 to 30 minutes."

caption: **Professional soccer players make sure they train to stay in peak condition.**

adidas

HEALTH AND RECOVERY

Professional soccer players are now aided by a wide arrangement of science and technology aimed at helping them compete. And they need it now more than ever. Top players on big clubs in Europe and South America are busier than ever during the season. In addition to league games, many teams also play in regional competitions such as the Champions League. Each country has its own cup tournament that runs throughout the season, adding more games. Plus, the very best players also play for their national teams, resulting in even more games.

This can lead to some of the top players being on the field for 50 to 60 matches a year. Playing that many matches can be tiring and lead to injuries. That is why players must go through the regeneration process after games to help their bodies recover.

"There has been a lot of research that has gone into using food as a form of recovery, whether that be different foods based on the time in the season, or the importance of getting the proper nutrients into your body within a window post-practice," Guter said. "It is all based on using food to recover from one session to get you ready for the next. . . .

Injuries can cause players to miss games or even seasons. Teams try to help their players prevent and recover from injuries.

Orange slices at halftime or postgame have been replaced by recovery shakes."

ENHANCING A SCOUT'S EYE

Technology is also changing the way players are coached. Coaches can't be everywhere at once. Technology helps them track how players are performing.

Instant replay technology allows officials to review controversial calls.

Professional soccer teams have a technical staff dedicated to tracking player performance. The biggest teams, such as those in the English Premier League, make detailed reports on each player. Team officials study the reports and use them to evaluate players every day.

But down in the seventh tier of English soccer, teams can't afford that many officials or other staff. Those clubs don't make very much money. Players on Leatherhead Football Club in Surrey, for example, often have to work other jobs in addition to playing soccer.

To help make up the gap, the team turned to artificial intelligence (AI) in 2019. The IBM company has an AI system called Watson. Watson can interpret all kinds of data, and its use for soccer was part of an experiment in 2019.

Watson takes in data by analyzing games and practices. It is able to call up data on demand. A coach could ask it to find video clips of penalty kick attempts by the team's strikers. Players can also review the data themselves, freeing up more time for the coaches.

VIDEO ASSISTANT REFEREE (VAR)

In 2012, after a number of controversial calls, instant replay using goal line technology was added to the Laws of the Game. This technology featured a chip in the ball that detected its position on the field and clearly indicated whether it had crossed the goal line. In 2016 replay was expanded with the use of a Video Assistant Referee (VAR). VAR is an extra official who assists the referee by reviewing plays on video.

Players are closely monitored while training to make sure they are ready for game day.

TRACKING MOVEMENT

Many people have devices, such as smartphones, that use data from Global Positioning System (GPS) satellites in order to track location and provide directions. But many soccer teams use data from GPS satellites too. Many professional teams have their players wear devices during games. These devices connect to GPS satellites. Each player is assigned his or her own specific device that tracks his or her movements while on the field. This data instantly appears on a computer. It can tell users how far the players have run, their top seeds, and the spots on the field where they spend most of their time.

This data is helpful for coaches and technical staff to analyze. They can see how hard a player is working. By understanding where on the field the player spends most of their time, coaches can learn if a player is or isn't tracking back on defense or where they are most effective. Other information such as heart rate can be vital for the trainers and athletic staff to watch a player to make sure they are healthy.

"We monitor every step that our players take, in training and in games," said Red Bull Salzburg head coach Jesse Marsch. "We believe that our young players are like Ferraris, and we want to make sure that they are carefully taken care of and monitored, so that they can play at top speed. We also analyze the opponent for weaknesses, and we attack in those areas with our aggressiveness and power."

SOCCERBOT 360

Red Bull Salzburg takes its training program very seriously. The club uses the latest technology to give its players an edge. One of the devices it uses is called SoccerBot 360. SoccerBot displays images on the walls surrounding a player that contain tasks for him to finish. For example, he may have to hit moving targets as a clock ticks. This helps players perform under pressure.

CHAPTER 4

SOCCER'S FINAL FRONTIER

Soccer has always been called a game of the people. That wasn't always the case, though.

Since soccer became popular in the early 1900s, it grew to become the most-played and most-watched sport in the world. Boys learned to play it at an early age, and men's club teams were passionately followed. The World Cup draws as many viewers around the world as the Olympics.

But for young women, opportunities to play the game they loved were harder to come by. Soccer was either not offered or was not an option for female players. All that changed in the 1970s when a new US law required schools to offer sports to both boys and girls. Recreational soccer took off in the United States. Girls helped make soccer the most played teenage sport in the country.

caption: **The World Cup is one of the most watched sporting events in the world. About 3.6 billion people tuned in during the 2018 World Cup.**

2018 FIFA WORLD CUP RUSSIA™

Men's soccer had a big head start on the women's game, though. The World Cup had been going on for more than 50 years before there was serious talk of a women's equivalent. Finally, at the 1986 FIFA Congress meeting, Norwegian FIFA representative Ellen Wille grabbed a microphone to advocate for women's soccer. Within two years, FIFA staged a practice tournament, and in 1991 the first FIFA Women's World Cup took place in China.

The United States won that first tournament, which received very little attention in the United States. But Team USA became the world's dominant team over the next 30 years, winning three more Women's World Cups behind exciting players such as Mia Hamm, Abby Wambach, and Alex Morgan.

The United States hosted the 1999 Women's World Cup and shattered attendance records for the previous two tournaments. The United States beat China on penalty kicks in the final, further amplifying the buzz about the tournament. An iconic goal celebration by Brandi Chastain, who scored the winning penalty kick, landed the defender on the cover of *Sports Illustrated* and on the front page of newspapers across the country.

Members of the US team celebrate after winning the 1999 Women's World Cup.

THE SLEEPING GIANT?

While the US women were having huge success, the men's team fell way behind. Contrary to its status throughout much of the world, professional soccer in the United States is still relatively new. Professional baseball, for instance, turned 150 years old in 2019. The National Football League celebrated

While the US men's team failed to qualify for the 2018 World Cup, the women's team went on to win the 2019 Women's World Cup.

a century of seasons the same year. MLS began in 1996, making it the youngest men's major league in the country.

Two years before MLS was launched, the United States hosted the World Cup. At the time, the view around the world of soccer in the United States was not a bright one. The Americans had qualified for the World Cup in 1990, the first time they'd played in the tournament in 40 years.

In 1994, however, the whole world saw that Americans not only loved soccer but could play the game. The World Cup in the United States set an attendance record that still stands today. And the US national team advanced to the second round of the tournament before losing to mighty Brazil. Brazil went on to win the World Cup for a record fourth time.

MAJOR LEAGUE SOCCER

As part of the agreement to host the World Cup, FIFA had one demand. The United States must establish a pro soccer league. The country had lacked one since the North American Soccer League (NASL) folded in 1984.

One of the key figures in creating MLS was Lamar Hunt. Hunt was an American soccer pioneer. He was an NASL investor and helped bring World Cup matches to his native Dallas. Hunt invested in two MLS teams and helped build the league's

THE LAMAR HUNT US OPEN CUP

First held in 1913–14, the US Open Cup is the second-oldest soccer tournament in the world. It is open to every men's soccer team in the United States. In 1999 Lamar Hunt's name was added to the tournament in honor of his contributions to American soccer.

first soccer-specific stadium for the Columbus Crew.

The World Cup helped introduce the soccer world to Americans. Tab Ramos of the United States was a creative playmaker and star of the World Cup. He became the first American to sign with MLS. The league added other stars from the tournament such as Colombia's Carlos Valderrama.

MLS had a good first year. Attendance was solid, and the production was very good overall. The American players developed and grew. Brian McBride of the Crew was a little-known player before the season started, but he became one of the top forwards in MLS. He eventually became a regular starter for the US national team in three World Cups.

The league survived a period in the early 2000s in which it had to eliminate two teams. But by 2020 it had grown to a league of 26 teams and counting. Though other sports are still more popular, MLS has carved out a unique and passionate fanbase.

Tab Ramos, *right*, was the first American signed by MLS.

NATIONAL WOMEN'S SOCCER LEAGUE

The United States has long been a leader in women's soccer. Establishing a pro league took some time, though. Two leagues came and went in the early 2000s. Finally, in 2013, the National Women's Soccer League (NWSL) debuted. It had more financial support than the previous leagues. This helped it overcome some of the challenges all new leagues face. The NWSL also built on the momentum of the US wins at the 2015 and 2019 Women's World Cups. Today the NWSL is one of the most competitive leagues in the world, and it has plans to continue adding more teams.

CHAPTER 5

TOOLS OF THE TRADE

Goodyear is perhaps best known today as a maker of tires. Charles Goodyear's vulcanization process for rubber helped revolutionize that industry. It also transformed how soccer balls are made.

In the early 1800s, balls were made from an inflated pig's bladder. Not only were these easy to puncture, they were irregularly shaped. The ball didn't roll very well.

When Goodyear made it easier to make rubber, it also became easier to make the liner of a soccer ball. Goodyear produced the first soccer ball made of vulcanized rubber in 1855. The ball was much rounder and stronger than anything that had come before.

Another problem with early soccer balls was they had stitching like an American football. The stitching often broke

caption: **Charles Goodyear invented the first vulcanized rubber soccer ball in 1855.**

after over 90 minutes of action. And the leather laces absorbed water, which made the ball heavy.

As a goalkeeper for the Denmark national team, Eigil Nielsen handled a lot of soccer balls. When he wasn't playing, he worked for a shoe company and handled a lot of leather. That led him to experiment with soccer ball design.

VANISHING SPRAY

Part of a referee's job is to make sure defenders are standing the required distance from the ball on free kicks. But players sometimes cheat forward. Referees today use a spray that marks a clear line on the grass and disappears later. This vanishing spray was invented by Brazilian Heine Allemagne in 2000. It made its World Cup debut in 2014.

In 1951 Nielsen designed the first soccer ball without laces. Then in 1962, Nielsen unveiled a ball that used 32 individual panels of leather. This created the classic soccer ball look that is known around the world. The Adidas company completed that look when it added alternating black and white panels on its 1970 Telstar model at the World Cup.

GETTING A GRIP

In a quarterfinal match at the 2004 European Championship, Portugal goalkeeper Ricardo needed to change his luck. The match with England had come down to a shootout, and the

Portuguese keeper had allowed five straight penalty kicks to zoom past him. With the match on the line, Ricardo decided to take off his gloves.

It might have been a coincidence, but Ricardo made a key save on England's next kick and Portugal won. Almost all keepers today play with gloves, but that was not the case until the 1970s.

Ricardo's famous gloveless save helped Portugal knock England out of the 2004 European Championship.

Goalkeeper gloves date back much longer. A soccer ball manufacturer came up with the idea for leather gloves for goalkeepers in 1885. But the first keeper to use them regularly was Amadeo Carrizo of Argentina in the 1940s and '50s. They became more popular as strategy evolved. Keepers began coming out to snare balls and pass them quickly to teammates. It helped to have a good grip on the ball.

Keepers wearing gloves became the norm in the 1970s. Today, those gloves are heavily padded and thick. But thanks to technological advancements, they are also very light. And gloves can be customized exactly to a player's wishes.

BOOT ROOM

In much of the soccer-playing world, soccer cleats are known as boots. They got that name because that is what they were in the early days. Soccer became popular in England among factory workers. They would head to play still wearing their work boots.

These boots didn't do much to keep a player upright. So players started hammering metal studs into the sole to get good traction. By the 1900s, shoes designed specifically for soccer were taking shape. These designs remained relatively simple until the 1950s.

Adi Dassler and his company Adidas released the first soccer shoe with molded plastic cleats.

German Adi Dassler was the son of a shoemaker. After making shoes for champion sprinter Jesse Owens at the 1936 Olympics in Berlin, Germany, Dassler and his brother Rudolf started an athletic shoe company. They later split, with Rudolf Dassler starting the company Puma and Adi starting Adidas.

In 1950 Adidas released the first soccer shoe with molded plastic cleats. The West Germany national team wore these cleats at the 1954 World Cup and won the tournament. The players credited their victory to their new shoes.

Modern soccer cleats are made of light, synthetic materials to help players move freely.

Players need comfortable, durable cleats to move and change directions quickly, especially on wet grass.

Soccer shoes have only gotten lighter and more advanced since then. Players need to cut quickly and don't want anything slowing them down. By 2020, many pro players wore cleats that weighed less than 0.25 pounds (100 g).

Much like the equipment it uses, soccer is a simple game. But there have been countless developments off the field that helped make the game so popular today. Modern soccer is the product of those innovations.

TIMELINE

1848

Students at Cambridge University in England write the first known set of rules that created the modern game of soccer.

1863

The Football Association is founded in England. Using some of the Cambridge Rules, the FA writes the first laws of the game.

1872

England and Scotland play the first international soccer match.

1904

FIFA forms in Paris to become the world's governing body of soccer.

1930

FIFA stages the first World Cup, an idea of president Jules Rimet.

1951

Eigil Nielsen invents the first soccer ball without laces.

1974

The Netherlands makes the World Cup final playing its total football style.

1991

FIFA holds the first Women's World Cup.

2010

Spain wins its first World Cup title playing its *tiki-taka* style of quick passes and movement.

2018

More than 3.5 billion people tune in for the final of the World Cup.

HONORABLE MENTIONS

ALL-SEATER STADIUMS

Standing-room-only sections called terraces used to be a common feature of soccer stadiums. That changed on April 15, 1989. Ninety-six people were killed at Hillsborough Stadium in Sheffield, England, after too many fans were allowed into a terrace. Fans were crushed against fencing surrounding the area. In response, the British government required all major stadiums to eliminate standing-room areas for safety.

THE PREMIER LEAGUE

In the 1980s, English soccer was in decline. Stadiums were aging, violence was common in the crowd, and the league was considered inferior to those of Italy and Spain. The top teams had to share profits with the rest of the league. In the early 1990s, five of these clubs formed a new league. The Premier League changed the world of pro soccer forever. Many observers consider it the best league in the world.

TIEBREAKERS

In 1968 Yosef Dagan watched in horror as his native Israel was eliminated from the Olympics after drawing 1–1 with Bulgaria. The way to settle ties at the time was to draw pieces of paper. Israel's captain pulled a paper saying "no" while Bulgaria received "yes" and that was that. Dagan proposed teams trade kicks from the penalty spot. Whoever made the most goals won. The exact format was approved starting with the 1970 World Cup, even though FIFA never gave Dagan the credit.

GLOSSARY

cup
A trophy or tournament.

defender
A player whose job is to keep the other team from taking shots and scoring.

dribble
To control and advance the ball with one's feet.

forward
Also called a striker, the player who plays nearest the opponent's goal.

free kick
An unguarded kick awarded to a team after an opponent's foul.

goalkeeper
A player whose primary duty is to prevent the ball from entering the net.

midfielder
A player who stays mostly in the middle-third of the field and links the defenders with the forwards.

offsides
An infraction that is called when a player is closer to the goal than the last defender (other than the keeper) when the ball is kicked.

penalty kick
A play in which a shooter faces a goalkeeper alone; it is used to decide tie games or as a result of a foul inside the penalty area.

pioneer
A person who was an important figure in his or her profession.

professional
A person who gets paid to perform.

MORE INFORMATION

BOOKS

Carothers, Thomas. *Women's World Cup Heroes*. Minneapolis, MN: Abdo Publishing, 2019.

Kortemeier, Todd. *Total Soccer*. Minneapolis, MN: Abdo Publishing, 2017.

Moussavi, Sam. *World Cup Heroes*. Minneapolis, MN: Abdo Publishing, 2019.

ONLINE RESOURCES

Booklinks
NONFICTION NETWORK
FREE! ONLINE NONFICTION RESOURCES

To learn more about innovations in soccer, visit **abdobooklinks.com** or scan this QR code. These links are routinely monitored and updated to provide the most current information available.

INDEX

ABOUT THE AUTHOR

Kristian R. Dyer has covered MLS since 2005 for outlets such as ESPN.com and the Athletic. In addition, he is a regular on the Red Bulls pregame broadcast on MSG Network. He played college soccer at Montclair State University. He lives in New Jersey with his wife and their son.